T0151982

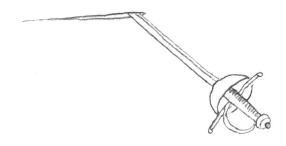

LISA ROBERTSON'S MAGENTA SOUL WHIP

Coach House Books

Toronto

Published with the generous assistance of the Canada Council for the Arts and the Ontario Arts Council. Coach House Books also acknowledges the support of the Government of Canada through the Book Publishing Industry Development Program.

LIBRARY AND ARCHIVES CANADA

CATALOGUING IN PUBLICATION

Robertson, Lisa
Lisa Robertson's magenta soul whip / Lisa Robertson.

ISBN 978-1-55245-215-8

I. Title.

PS8585.O3217L58 2009   C811'.54   C2009-900013-X

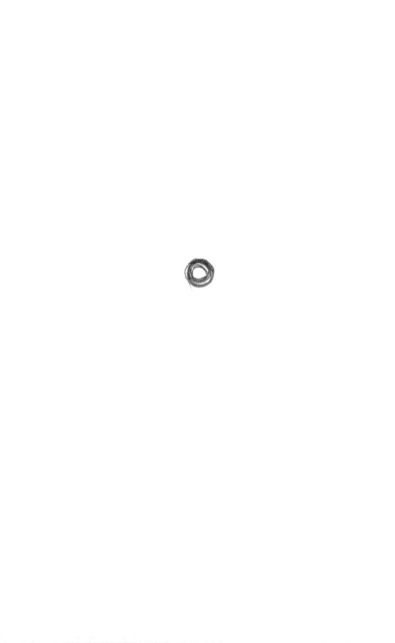

Lucite

(an amuse-gueule)
(because the present is not articulate)

Sit us on Lucite gently and we will tell you how knowledge came to us.

First the dull mud softened, resulting in putrefaction, lust and intelligence, pearl globs, jewelled stuff like ferrets, little theatres of mica, a purse containing all the evil smells of daily life. Then just the one vowel, iterate and buttressed and expiring; leaning, embracing, gazing. With our claw it devised identity for the sake of food. Selves, it says, feeding us, I adore you, you know. Like a boy blowing from a tree, we decided, we were paid, we were free. We incessantly prepared for the future. On the title page, two angels blowing on the trumpets of fame held up a globe decorated with three fleurs-de-lys and topped with a crown. We learned habits and tricks. We were a single grin with lips pasted back. We said we saw Europes of hallucination, fatty broths sprinkled with deer, stencilled eagles, serpents and lurid rags. That was a format of saying, a frayed ligature. We were fading into the presence or absence of food.

Enough of the least. Sincerity takes too long in an aggressive emergency. Also we feel a sense of duality. We wear out the art. We start to modify our vocables – flick, pour, dribble estrangement's sex. Since it is we who are one, and we who are scattered. We're this pair or more which can't absorb one another in a meaning effect. We feel palpitated by daylight and its deliberate plants. We feel this elsewhere sculpt our body.

We would be walking down the street in the city. Gauze would be everywhere. The day would be big, halting, gracious, revocable, cheap. We'd be the she-dandies in incredibly voluptuous jackets ribboning back from our waists, totally lined in pure silk, also in pure humming, and we'd be heading into the buildings with ephemera like leafage or sleeves or pigment. The streets are salons that receive abundantly our description. The buildings are charming. And our manners are software. We feel sartorial joy. We'd be at the river watching the fat water on the blond built part, loving temporal improprieties, the bright trash floating in slow liberation. We'd be applying our makeup at noon, leaning on the balustrade, thinking about a little shun, a little fight, a little sofa. We'd be thinking about hinges. We'd feel for our pen. Something might seduce us. A likeness. A knowledge.

Samesame pouring through it.

Early Education

I designed my own passivity. I present it to you by my face, by your guts, and in the name of human space. I was born into a rough little city, site of hasty invention actively dissolving into steel sky. The city was a glittering ruin sucked upwards.

I

great virtues are numerous and wisdom has a laughable magnitude. the circumference of a human creature is his own testimonium, her superb mortal resistance as a creature is a liquid gate. our hearts are intelligible. to excite and to tempt you I will relate the ways of my past unhappiness. should I invoke necessity or fate? quomodo item I invoke is unbelievable. all gods are gravegods. what is without predicate? let's sing to the god who requires it. let's sing to our enemies also. quæram te, invocans te et I'll invent credens in te: a predicate is a noble enemy and my fidelity is my own disaster, inspirasti mihi per feeling humanitatem with this speech.

(Another version of the same beginning is simpler and more direct: in the long science of submission it is the mind that, quietly spectacular, unhooks the bodies and opens the face.)

II

the dominator is cuddled inside me: what would you call that? when we quibble and feast, what would you call that? since tua quidquid fades, has faded, this quidquid that's your name. all that's feral in me, whatever being I am, eats into my docent. I invoke dominance to undo myself.

I had no enemies, no parent, no clock. dominant you filled the nurse's tits and so abundantly taught me to sip. I'm telling you about things I don't remember, nothing more, fibbing and sipping, sipping and fibbing, very similar. et cum non intellecto me obsessit, non subditus indignation, no servitude. quam scientes is my nutrient. dominant qui est semper vivus and nothing in us tu creasti et really instabilium et immutable. quam illa intra visceral matrix? dominant my soft word, no memoria could have prepared me for your earth. I am the first suckling among multa, your artifice, your animal, gaudy with cries, gaudy with hunger and lovely with hunger and hunger.

III

listen to the humans fib. misery dictates. I remember the fibs of my infancy, a fib per heartbeat cooked by earth. will this commemorate me? dominant do you remember me?

my ego's made from milk, abundant fountains of milk, my dominant, my own, which dedicate themselves to the illuminant corpus, instructress of senses, so that I speak to you in the syllables of your name dominant and as bonus I make for you a nest of my ordinary thighs, tu, forma omnia et lege.

ergo dominant for you I have the fidelity of a fox a piglet an enemy a name multum so many fidelities and oblivions for you are shadow and concept with no memory no vestige no need.

IV

remember the undulant speech of your childhood enemy saying give it give it give it? I give it as various vocables and membranes voluntarily like this I name the liquids and seconds that move the body turning towards memory and emitting sound among its quorum this turning and opening this masking and what gets called humanæ vitæ authors no greater horror.

So who possesses the stamina to parent their own sensibility? no brat does and beneath the school of belts a language its audibility no refuge, no accident. to be coherent is to form enemies. dominant I wanted to wear memory like a moulded hunger willing ahead of myself some form of satisfaction or

vindicate legendary torment with what certainty did I console
my welts.

V

though dominant even my fibs are ordinary as belts flicking
against authority a peccadillo diligently diligently unspeakable.

a kid's weaned on eternal promises and humiliation. dominant
give me your superb sign so I can use it as a crutch or a rope
cast into my pointless fidelity, yes dominant I'll tell each
dilated fib with my dripping tongue as delicious recreation,
enstate my credo of necessity, the tongue like an ego to me,
dominant – whom shall I serve? without you for whom welts
fatten I'd be minus agency minus glory minus number my
author who cuddles me insatiably my soul's bulky with you as
it is bulky with fibs.

VI

whatever the cause of the grace of dogs, the soft odour of
books, the quibbling of kids, it's unbearable. no docent knows
such grammar. nor am I parsed, me, a vain wreath of
milk, vanity itself, caro factum, quia certiones, non spiritus

ambulans and islands of written stuff, a vast itinerary of errors
as I died upwards towards you, vita mea, like a magnet, sure,
like girls die of fierce love and friezes commemorate the fierce
cords of light that are their souls and soldiers eat sponge cake
and I don't love you and I fornicate towards you singing
down down and it is the solemn world I pull against my
tummy, down down and no fierce extreme sedates me no
sequence of the lips and teeth.

say nothing of the soul that flutters its sleeve dictating not this
not that not this muddled doctrine. I'll not name each obliv-
ion each venal carthage each dumb rut written up in verse.
dominant my ink's not diligent like yours. I simply tug and
vend and strum at pacts secundum signa quibbling litteris in
commodo. sit poetica stupid with words past their sweet-
arsed date.

it is the difficult tally of my tongue to admit that such songs
and those of puerile docents stroked my milky ego.

VII

dominant may I call you rex now and feed you tidbits? my
heart calls you rex because you're my first part, as rex I'll serve
you what are called tidbits and each locution and scribble and

number just adores you rex what is vanity is really your discipline for vanis peccata delectum multa for the rest of my life to please you I won't fib rex, I promise.

and towards what illusion my little rex do I tighten the cord that is my ink and adulate everything sentient. rex my pet what is suspended between us is sewn of figura.

who can resist a Human? who doesn't finger lies?

VIII

a word's a precious vase to sip from, an illicit verb. both kids and scholars sip there the sweet lubricity spilling over tongue and rex I sipped also I can safely say this now since I sip from you no other figment no other persona no other sentence rex what is suspended between us

the soldier reaches from behind the falling man's neck to grasp his snout; he is becoming a horned animal.

The Story

On the eastern sky, fingers of pink light.
Facing the sun we left town and drove, fresh
light on our arms. A young girl slept under
the opening fingers. But what can we
keep. All night they sleep. We launch into rest
and the flames burn through
alone in its clearing. The brave thing would be
to sleep in a hut again, dawn to nervy
dark, studying
the ground. A covey of women got out
worn and tough. So much for that.

And all night long the truck sheared through the
night into the dawn. And the sun went down
and all the roads grew dark. And here I lay
in ambush all night. In quiet Sleep my
eyes shut. I lay down and slept
in luxury. I went to Sleep above
the wash of ripples. Dawn came. By night we
ran onward. Nine days I drifted. Sleep weighed
on my eyes. And I went to rest out of
the wind. I slept on duty. Day waned.

All the roads grew dark. I cut, I died, I
fell, I dove, I ate, I fell, I fed, I
felt, and there I lay in ambush. I fought
I found, I fled, I flung, I flew, I fore
bore, I forbade, I forgot and my eyes
my eyes shut. I lay down and
shut. I forgave, I forsook, I got, I
lay down and slept in luxury. I hid
in luxury. I went to Sleep before
I hurt. I kept, I knew, I laid.
I left, and went to Sleep above
the wash of ripples. I lent, I let
the wash of ripples. Dawn came. By night we
lay. I lost, I made, I met, I over
came, I overdid, and dawn came
above the wash of ripples
ran onward. Nine days I drifted. Sleep weighed,
ran onward. I ran, I said, I saw, I
sought, I sold, I sent, I set, I shook, and
on my eyes nine days drifted.

I shut, I sang, and Sleep weighed on my eyes.
I went to rest out of the wind. Into the dawn
I thrust. Day waned. I sunk, I sat
I slew, I slept, I slid into evening

to rest out of the wind. I spent, I span
I wept until Sleep came. And
I stunk. And I slept on duty. I struck
hid in darkness, dropped
my eyes and nodded, overcome.
I swore, I took, I taught, I tore, I told
I wrote. Day waned into evening.

Burnt, I burst, I cast, I chid day, waned
into evening. I crept, I crept, I
dared, I dug, I dipt, I drew, I dreamt
two hours had disappeared.
I dwelt, I wept until Sleep came. I froze.
I gelt, I girt, I grew, I hung, I helpt
I hewed, I knelt and I resumed.

And all the roads grew dark
with my longing and my tears. It snowed
in darkness. I strewed, I strove, I swelled all night.
The truck sheared through the Night.

A Hotel

(after Oscar Niemeyer)

I will take my suitcase into a hotel and
Become a voice
By studying stillness and curtains

I will take my stillness into a hotel
Careening, not flowing, through
Cities become his voice

Into a hotel I will take my city
And roads
And the entire moving skin of history

Utopia is so emotional.
I'm speaking of the pure sexual curves
Of utopia, the rotation
Of its shadows against the blundering
In civitas. History does not respond
To this project – History, who has disappeared into
Architecture and into the
Generosity of the dead. This states
The big problem of poetry. Who could
Speak for the buildings, for the future of the dead
The dead who are implicated in all
I can say? On this very beautiful surface
Where I want to live
I play with my friends
Like they do down there.
I don't understand what I adore.
I think of my body in the night
And remember my grandparents. With
Blood running through my wrists I represent
This. I believe my critique of devastation
Began with delight. Now what surprises me
Are the folds in political desire
Their fragile nobility, Sundays of
Rain. Listening to music, things pass.
I cry softly thinking of friendships then
Begin again to invent the line of
My life amidst utopia. Probably

This is the centre – the worn-out house, walls

Humming the repose of systems, the

Modest light, but I wanted an urgent

Line to begin the future, something like you,

What will you do with your legs and your heart?

Some think only of pleasure in their projects.

I am one of those people

Or so desire. I needed to make a living

So provoked astonishment. What I said

Is already gone, locked in

Migration. Sometimes we make things that seem

To have will – yet the beautiful life of

The house is each day more fragile. We suffer

And laugh and swim. We go

Daily to the botanical gardens to witness

Complication. Each plant becomes what we

Love in its other language as we rest

Near the privacy of women. I wait patiently with this voice

At this late hour, in our rudimentary

Lodgings, in our migrations, and the future

Is terrible and is a play

Of liberty. Work that ignores the night

Is not my work. I'll solicit nothing

But ornament, that spacious edifice –

Kinds of ornament are change

Because it will change anyway

Beside the privacy of women

When I'm with them I forget
The simplest fact
Of loneliness which is not regret
I will take my privacy
Into its hotel.

After Trees

The season is called evening.
Out of belief come men
and then the sea and then the air
and then the upper part ignites
and a child comes screaming rosy fluids
and then the mother sleeps and what is change

World prim or corpulent such that
I don't want to know
that the spirit world is behind everything and full of shapes

For the idea of earth rumpling the air
the sun fountaining its hot light
the lake tarnished slightly by vapours
the grass all pearled-up with wetness from the earth
the eye rotating with bodies
bodies pouring life to the depth of what we can feel
and then its retreat
for the silent face
space silent around it
I cried

This is called anything
And Lucretius is a girl.

what's

    a vestige

what's

    an ego

what's

    grace

what locution helps this soft stove's dreamt scrap
in fracas? Love, be my believable
tutor. Figurine, govern this redundant
flush. Fate, resemble superlative and
solemn congress. Holy animal, be
Luck. Be force of anything earthlike and
lovely and limited. Footstar, ear, give
credence

It is a fact that it is in the nature of gods
to enjoy their immateriality in a place of
profound peace. They know nothing of our business
and are quite detached. No pain or trouble
tests them – they don't need our experience.
Sometimes I permit myself to travel
in their vitality. Their posture and noise
pertain to History. When they lose their will

I feel love
mixed with repulsion

Anyway, however diffident, my goal
is tranquility
emitted in a stream
and widely diffused
as if by a wind
but my body keeps confessing to me
of existence and humility –
such extravagance incites my measure
or I should say inflates
as with an acrid perfume
wood enlivens
gold fog, fattening branches, wilderness of
inscribed space, the cities blooming with kids

Two paths lead to the body
– the peacock mewls into rain –
a liquid rope attaches them.
Rocks and animals weep and tree roots
reel into society. It's sound that ripens
the fruit. These are the two paths: liquid
and sound. They have no number.
My industry dissolves when I think of this

Therefore livid as an animal I peruse
the long world that flares with souls
no other victory is possible
just this potent ration
I'll take to the terminus by foot
and leave folded under the sky when I go

The elements too are somewhat rationed
but they host our least excitement
as well as weather, misery and solemnity.
There is nothing else – only their wrong use
each tender filament cries out
I want to copy this with my hands

My own ignorance has to do with
this luminous pocket I've arrived in
as through a secret knothole
with the same flowers Homer chose
and his verse is my body
turning like a vase of anemones

Equipped with such formidable mortality
whatever style I choose operates in me like a sky –
it passes and changes and persists and I possess nothing
but the sum of naming, curious and
frantic.
The nascent category flits complicate.
Fear shades it.
I mean the exulted creation called fear
which is also curious
and raw and turbulent and opens

The names release birds and animals
into wild chance. Fruit trees
don't stop changing either – each thing
ripens its own space
and the determined light flows around our bodies
so we become cormorants and gulls
with new senses

Furthermore each call flowers.
Seasons erupt from the syllables
so persuasively
the luminous effort seems to annul
Chance, which next appears in the distance
tender, hesitant, turning to its name like an animal
before it moves towards the forest
and its strange work

In this poem Lucretius appears as a girl
on a rock
sunning and twisting

It transpires that murmurs and clickings

Are nature to each body

Sound never resolves itself

And what we hear erupts into other senses

Or perhaps it sways like a footbridge

Even our hands dream of stuff

They dream of pigments and fruit trees and puzzles

They dream of the honey that escapes from our work

Then everything begins to dilate

The ingenious sea invents

All my incertitude

When I wake to the horizon-scrim at night

I forage obedient

The rolling substance
is not empty. Across rocks
abundance, the trunks
and branches of trees, vocal
to the bone
this sibilant anything
seized in the lightest and most plunging part
dares
the passage of my body
and amongst bodies, weight
pressed upwards from dirt
dedicates itself to habit
which is a god mixed with what we can want

What about the data of trees before
Virgil? The day comes out of the earth like
an animal and it goes. A suite of
shadow follows. Some of you don't have to
like it. Absence is a sauce licked up, a
little peplum of fat and lint flung
off. For today only
I'll accomplish novelty's capaciousness

So long
Figtree
Especially.

First Spontaneous Horizontal Restaurant

(after Lucretius)

'The cry of the flesh is not to be hungry, thirsty or cold; for he who is free of these and is confident of remaining so might even vie with Zeus for happiness.'

– Epicurus

Note: In order not to be hungry I made a restaurant. I made a broth. I made a perishable structure of comportment shaped by the synæsthesia of eating.

Here we linger and nibble, according to the shapes of need. Perhaps the restaurant tests the possible relations of chance to need. Perhaps it re-syncopates need and thriving. It poses a nutritive situation rather than a volume. The restaurant is a receiving device. It asks: What precisely is required in the moment? I want to study the refreshing flora within resistance. I want to relax also. I want health and resistance to tarry in synæsthesia. I want to move on. Thus I am thrown headlong into transcendent things.

Lucretius said that to flourish we must absorb more than we exude
Of elements, minerals and so forth.
We call this food, and it fabricates us
From the inside. But much does drip and escape
From the corporeal tissues and we use this
Excess to make belief.
It is normal therefore for the body to perish
From incessancy of belief. In the meantime
How about a milky pablum, nutmeats
Quickened with liquor, the iron
Our blood sucks from roots, the delicate
And ingenious bodies we call pastries
Or most intimate aspects of animals
Honey, sap and other lucky seepage
Various salts and the slightly bitter textures of leaves:
From a fortuitous concourse of atoms
Blond foams, dripping vineyards, these curved
Spontaneously out of the pleasurable earth.
Clots of rubbish washed up on shore became us.
Similar yet unrelated swerves hosted each
Fruit and flouncing pasture, which now with meagre effort
We're hard pressed to husband.
We use up the cattle and their fields. We use up iron.
Dirt's tired of giving. We sigh at our expired
Work, envious at the luck of our
Parents. We walk to the bar again with stooped shoulders.

Some say the soul is made of wind
Others say it's full of blood. They
Are certain and don't need this information.
Some, shut out of their homes by
Politics and circumstance, far from their
Siblings, flayed by grief, continue to
Pace through their ritual acts, judging
And proving. Bad luck wakes others up
To actual voices vibrating in torn open
Breasts. They are hungry.
Why should the fear of death feed them?
Why do we tip over the supper tables
Of both cousins and strangers? We must transform
What we are in hunger.

Lucretius says the soul, the speaking, thinking force that flows
     through a girl
Is part of life not less than hand, foot or eyes are vital.
He says that thought is of the hungry
Body, not different than limbs and senses.
He says fragility sustains us. I mean
Even in effortful situations there is a delay
A minimal interval where we turn towards hurt.
This delay could be consistent
With deep reverence
Without cause.

Say the girl or animal again wakes up
Desiring unctuous bouillons and summer Latin
Of incredible lightness and smoothness
Incredible fineness and smoothness
In a kind of direction both up and down
Since she suddenly knew this to be absent.
Say there is a surplus
Of speculation.
In this way we are not restricted to only falling.

Let's take the totality of an animal.
Some bone, blood in the veins, heated fluid of the gut
Nerves weaving a form
Fattening some method
Finally you see corpulent colour, tasting
And absorbing dirt, and a language suspends itself as if falling.
Any correction is arbitrary, monstrous.
Now, attend to veritable hunger.
Something astonishingly fresh might approach
Reveal its wild fragrance. Every ease
Was first unbelievable, outside, stunning
Seeking admiration. Then it becomes the colour of the sky
With its various startling components.
Everything is for the first time mortal
Improvised, surging to the look.
Nothing else foams towards me.

Nobody lifts their eyes to

No romantic, impracticable, extravagantly ideal conditions

No impossibly ideal schemes

No impossibly ideal, visionary, chimerical perfection having
        no human location

Silly, inevitable, hot elsewhere coming

To the scale of no parties, no past, no other

In danger and alarm.

The institution of social longing fell

Nowhere, in no direction, neither to the side of

The left nor the right, nor up high, nor lowering, limitlessly

Towards an uncertain site intemperate

In no determined direction of space and in no determined time

In no untimely place it moves

A thing crying itself by resorting to light

And then to take hold of semblance and call it

Nothing as dirt is zapped through

With habit and lacking a better verb I promote

This inauthenticity and the earth is a tipping dish

Where chance flings its messed-up items

Entirely apart from intention. Finally some

Combination happens to originate an appetite

And we are still

Rotating

On

Doubt.

How did we come to negation?

A Spontaneous Horizontal Restaurant begins where Utopia ends.

Lucretius invented it in Book Two.

You have to realize that elsewhere a parallel materiality also
spontaneously resists our will.

Place here the catalogue of hungers.

Call it the future.

Wooden Houses

A work called wooden houses begins
It explores different degrees of fear.

And it is curious that you did not choose a secular image
Augustine's own task was equally impossible.

And we said a boat would come and take you to Venice
And you are a law of language.

And my mouth took part
And we fed you morphine mixed with honey.

And you are a rare modern painting in the grand salon
And you are a wall of earth.

And you are an ideological calm
And you are flung out to search.

And you are framed only by the perspectival rigours of masonry
And you are not a neutral instrument.

And you are pornographic
And you are the imagination of society as a tree.

And you are the kneeling woman who expresses some alarm
The woman looks somewhat apprehensively at the viewer.

And you are the pronoun of love, scorn, accusation, glamour
Everything you know about the animal pertains to the riot of love.

And you are Torontos of cold trees
Where erupts the morning's catalogue.

And you did not die outside of love
And you do not judge.

And you roll down scrabbling at its glaze
The man on the right runs away terrified.

And you see how an animal dies
Giving a first drop of voluptuousness.

And you seem to pour rosewater
Leaning on trees for rest.

And you speak in leaves
To flirt and fight and appease.

And you turn into a her not knowing what's happening
The woman in your midst may be kneeling or seated or may
    simply be drawn out of scale.

And you are the last wooden house
The carved frame includes the heads of dogs.

And you will not die
But chance is always a little ahead.

And your failure is my tongue
The dramatic effect is heightened by the bright red ground
        showing through the top layers.

And your heart broke off into this great desire to see
Into the tall grass.

And your plump arms emerge from the gold and rose-pink
        folds of your tunics
As in the ancient literary genres.

Because it is a known fact
The wounded fall towards the point.

Because of mute desire
You are the teak pavilion.

Because you wanted to be flattered
You are portrayed as the sea goddess Thetis with two of her
        five sons.

Chance is always a little ahead

But not under circumstances of its own choosing.

Emptying your apartment during the season of apricots
This wasn't true.

Genial then light
I tell mine complaint.

I tell mine complaint
I tell mine complaint.

I took part in the savage transaction
It burns to come back to you.

It is pure surface
It pushes straight towards the author of its hurt.

It was 3:04 a.m.
Like you invented summer in a text I discovered in your
drawer in the summer of 1998.

Or a woman whose complete being seems to sing sex
One man shows his companion.

Sometimes the most ample designations are so stifling you
can only go further inside
Supposing a designation to have an interior.

The fabric is knotted to reveal your figure
The folds suggest the roundness of a young girl.

The tissue is syllables and dreams in a distant colony
The parts of life are not happening in tandem.

Then it is summer
This material is reconciled to chance, which is spacious.

To make livid a philosophy
We helped you leave breath.

Whether love comes as a young boy with girlish limbs
You are behind and between Christ and the adulteress,
     witnessing.

You are buckled into my truth
A young woman looks openly out of the picture.

You are the claustrophobia of the image
At its peak a couple stare at the lightning-filled sky.

You are the exhausting pace of boredom versus the use of
     the body
You are the next cabin also.

The figures represent the four ages of man
You call this passivity.

You left the books that had surrounded you and me holding
     your body
Accompanied by the city.

You lie there wounded
You see the precision of the distant city through the round
     arches of the bridge.

You see the women's thick hair bound with coloured ribbons,
     their complicated sandals and the sprigs of olive
You slip your cock into the actress's vagina.

You thrum and click
You took part in the savage transaction of negation.

You are wooden houses transformed into apartments and
     restaurants
Your breath thrummed the wooden house.

Your failures are no longer sacred.

Draft of a Voice-Over for Split-Screen Video Loop

'A young woman looks openly out of the picture.'

'A young woman looks openly out of the picture.'

'Her experience of scale is always paradoxical.'

'As for the unconscious, she is breathing in its Latin.'

'Philosophy comes from her having difficulty.'

'Her experience of scale is always paradoxical.'

'When girls were flowers this wasn't true.'

'Her pronoun is sedition unrecognized as such.'

'The women is itself not a content.'

*'Her voice turns towards weakness and shame and it pours down
her face.'*

'When it comes to flowers, she is parody.'

'How does she represent herself as thinking?'

'So what if she is thick and stupid behind her life. It is not private.'

'It can't be regulated.'

'No, it is a survival, a learning-to-live.'

'Knowledge is truth until it's ordinary.'

'To super-add girls speaking to humans is not a pleasure.'

'No, it is a survival, a learning-to-live.'

'Probably whatever the feminine might mean has to do with the intellectual relationship to change.'

'None of the forms feel big enough.'

'She imprecisely uses freedom.'

'Part of her wanted nothing.'

'She will be the pronoun of her analysis.'

'Philosophy comes from her having difficulty.'

'When women are exiled it seems normal.'

'Probably whatever the feminine might mean has to do with the intellectual relationship to change.'

'She thinks she undoes her femininity to give herself pleasure.'

'She brings this vocabulary into her mouth to sex it.'

'The information of her fear is her most serious and fragile part.'

'She doesn't have much time to understand her mortality.'

'Her voice turns towards weakness and shame and it pours down her face.'

'She exploited a splitting at the level of process.'

'Her pronoun is sedition unrecognized as such.'

'She feels free to set out in any discourse.'

'She doesn't have much time to understand her mortality.'

'She hasn't been human.'

'She wants to tell about it but not necessarily in language.'

'She imprecisely uses freedom.'

'She says space is doubt.'

'She recycled the discarded part.'

'She exploited a splitting at the level of process.'

'She says space is doubt.'

'Part of her wanted nothing.'

'She smoothes her hair.'

'She recycled the discarded part.'

'She spirals wildly away.'

'She writes against herself.'

'She taught herself to make distinctions.'

'She writes against those who know how to read.'

'She thinks she undoes her femininity to give herself pleasure.'

'As for the unconscious, she is breathing in its Latin.'

'She wants to tell about it but not necessarily in language.'

'None of the forms feel big enough.'

'She will be the pronoun of her analysis.'

'She smoothes her hair.'

'She writes against herself.'

'She spirals wildly away.'

'She writes against those who know how to read.'

'She feels free to set out in any discourse.'

'So what if she is thick and stupid behind her life. It is not private.'

'She brings this vocabulary into her mouth to sex it.'

'The information of her fear is her most serious and fragile part.'

'Thus she arrives at the idea of the mistake.'

'The masterpiece of her mouth feels natural.'

'The masterpiece of her mouth feels natural.'

'The women is itself not a content.'

'What the political will be to her cannot yet be quantified.'

'This is a concept.'

'She hasn't been human.'

'Thus she arrives at the idea of the mistake.'

'This is a concept.'

'To super-add girls speaking to humans is not a pleasure.'

'It can't be regulated.'

'What the political will be to her cannot yet be quantified.'

'Knowledge is ordinary.'

'When women are exiled it seems normal.'

The Stricture

'The 69 heads of Messerschmidt cast in lead are not heaven.'
'The magnetic cures of Mesmer on the plastic soul are more
    difficult to characterize.'
'The heavens of Flanders are like textile in lustrousness –
    a bridal textile.'
'We see the classic theme of a woman suffering, with pearl-
    sized nipples, pink cotton billowing or nacrous skin
    sprouting feathers.'
'Here is a perfume burner of Khorasan, a bird sitting on top.'
'Birds perch on heaven habitually. They are not certainty-
    seekers.'

I wanted to think into the stricture of appearances.

There was a time when I came close.

To help the problem I changed into a clematis, I changed into
    a dog, I changed into a perfumed smoke.

Some of my organs were outside history, which gave me an
    advantage.

Place here the idea of a necessary inconspicuousness.

'This is wrong'
'This is beautiful'
'This is social'
'This is not thinking'

It is the handiwork of appearing only.

This is the topic we discussed in your kitchen this winter.
I said I didn't know what thinking is.
You said you were trying to understand your sense of an
    inner voice, which was separate from thinking.
I didn't understand.
I let myself go blank.

I began by taking everything that was doubtful and throwing
    it out, like sand.

About 1836

(an essay on boredom)

I met a dog who collected doubt
until doubt offered a repose.
I met a dog who displayed as love
a surplus of inactivity.
A surplus of inactivity.
I asked the dog
what I should do about believing.
'Nothing' he replied.
He was the dog of Latinity
and non-knowledge.
Tacit dog I said
tell me about boredom.
The dog replied:

'At the edges of the villages of Europe
'there is boredom.
'The villages of Europe
'don't want your thinking.
'They want
'not a world.
'In these villages
'one rereads the soiled timetables

'of minor trains

'and finds therein

'Grace. This is called

'an environment. Now

'you weep its surplus.

'Nowhere is like that.

And the dog said

'I am going to call it hegemony when

'waking life

'feels like

'purchasing water.

'On animality I'll claim

'I wanted to go right out over wordlessness until it became
        a fabric

'and then to lick it

'gravely.

'At the same time I was chagrined

'and the social gadgetry hissed.

'The outside spread without is the village, the outside

'spread within is boredom.

'We are often mistaken about origins

'(against which we animals sleep).

'So I became a collector of things
'– ideas perhaps –
'smoothing them in the privacy of my ennui
'(my studio I mean)
'as they smooth their
'waning orchids.
'Genially I am an object.
'In my canine memory
'things gently combine –
'the glitter, the champagne, the sky-blue boudoirs
'distributed across a surface
'they would change but nothing would change
'ever ever ever.
'Time had no measure
'other than enjoyment and boredom.
'Simple bodies in combinations made types –
'one suffocating, one airy, one narcotic:
'there was an illegible relation to materiality
'and this was mistaken for orthodoxy
'but the orthodoxy did not replace the transcendent.
'In its radical æther
'flew
'some dandiacal cravat.

'One must withdraw for a long time to arrive at the minimum
'at the cosmological minimum.

'It takes an inhuman patience

'to make the erotic into itself.[†]

'By cosmology I mean

'out in the shadows, out at the edge of the parking lot, just beyond

'the signage, and beyond the erotic even

'one's relationship to utopia is elegiacal.

'Time there is other time.

'Forget the nostalgia for singularity. The

'dismantling of hegemony begins with boredom.

'If just a single one of the new sciences

'had been sacrificed to the livid boulevards

'(one of which extends from the era of Greek philosophy

'to the advent of Christianity)

'and the boulevard itself a mobile village –

'and so it is with our own past:

'Late Autumn

'Low Latin

'the history of the use of boredom

'remains latent.

'One's strategies – how should I put this –

'used up knowing.

_____

[†]   (as when a swallow flies into my room – when a swallow
       flies into my study – being delicate
       and light as their bodies are light
       they are entirely free of trouble.)

'I wanted to feel discourse on my pelt

'but all I could see was theology's iced hips

'contra the use of the present.

'Not will they welcome

'the concept, not

'the concept … (that being what one usefully does against
    loneliness).

'Whereas we in the villages, we must share our nightingales.

'Somebody brackets their body and somebody

'doesn't bracket their body.

'Each thing changes into a bare unit of wit

'which offers a repose at best.

'Excellent the applause excellent the money's

'boat-like gliding

'coming into peregrination

'to the point where all of the furnishing and utensils

'love one out of despair

'or lie

'with a filthy laugh.

'Soon there will be only society

'and caricature. Monsieur, I am frightened.

'My friends die.

'As for the river

'the light was the light. The surface

'imperceptible.

'Suicides and stories became trees.

'Was one for the event? Or on the wrong bridge?

'We do not pray. The brooder is thinking.

'The famed impossibility of repetition

'places itself in relation to

'the mercantile, hygienic and military class

'where those purchasers are honoured.

'Two elements accost one:

'both doors remain closed.

'The historian captures above all a document

'as if his eye loves.

'Experiments along these lines

'having a degree of luxury sufficient

'to a certain stage of myth

'– as in a letter to one's mother –

'elegantly dressed and rifle in hand

'(rifle not-yet-conscious) …

'And what does fashion determine?

'Fashion determines empathy.

'When one speaks to flowers for example

'it is an empathy one seeks and offers

'as when you offer thinking to a lily

'and it to you. But now we take a more humble view –

'some elements of divinity are simulacra

'and any theory of photography has a defeated and retreating
       feeling

'like certain cities one has left.

'One is not certain if boredom is emotion or philosophy or style
'thus its suppleness
'(whence fluorescence
'and flower tropes).
'Which leads to a kind of … material negative
'as recited on the ancient porches.

'One's torso swaddles Naught
'only the structure of sex
'its boat-like gliding.

'Whatever records the fabric of the heavens and the earth
'whatever cosmopolitan falcon
'in the inscription-splattered panic
'in the structure of waiting and epistemological
'catalogues, erotic problems –
'one can preserve the appearance of moving
'to mask an entire incompatibility with the present.
'An important part of the fabric of love is boredom
'and this is not social – it is the necessary repose
'of the socius: Nothing
'of machination, only the animal infinite
'contrapuntal, climbing the morning …
'What falcon's secular, most pliant
'tether snaps
'into dandiacal utterance
'until the bells ring queasily.

'In love one perceives directly using one's hormones and
        one's stupidity
'one's trifles that is – transcendence intact
'rigorous in the decoration of all belief
'as if sequestered in a hotel
'(hotel of the decor of precious origins).
'One slips all of one's desire into the small silken pocket deep
        in the cummerbund
'but leaves them their
'tuxedos –
'and this is fragility
'taking leave of itself
'Monsieur.

'Can we awake from the century already
'or only cast over it
'propositions about the political
'as if to rescue ourselves?

'Further to cosmology
'as the hawk shat
'who can say what commodity is
'if not the capacity to admit chance
'with no admonishment

Said the dog.

'Repeatedly, in a pattern
'what one thinks of the cosmos
'is nothing
'contra the misuse of the present
'and the texture of waiting.
'Sift ad hoc time or curse it
'one seems to understand scale
'(I mean in the cosmological sense)
'only ever in relation to chance.

'Simply to scaffold being
'in multiple frames of probability
'then swag it in heavy drapes –
'was that the timely choral work?
'Or rather that the question of time
'sat on the surface of language
'and laughed when I tried to face it.
'And laughed when I tried to face it.

'To turn from this institution
'in the position of not-believing:
'This would be the utopian turn.
'I can't do it.
'So I pierce utopia
'with divine boredom.
And then the dog – for it was a dog who spoke –
gently ambled off

betwixt black trunks of trees

and I am going to tell you that this dog

glanced back in simple sadness

said

'Soon there will be only society.'

A Modest Treatise

(an essay on perspective for Allyson Clay)

It was a warm September evening.

I dissolved corporeally into air leaving only my look.

The night was populated with images.

Some were moved easily to pity.

Some were sharp and suspicious, some credulous and pure.

Some were haughty and bitter.

Some human.

Some malleable and obsequious.

Some were gay.

Some were shy, solitary and austere.

Some liked to be praised by our work.

Some suffered when criticized.

Some were cruel in their arrogance, weak in danger and so forth.

It was a warm September evening and I entered its spaciousness,
    which was not classical.

It was pleasant to violate the canons of proportion.

It was pleasant to imagine their life.

I placed my body in relation to their mystical privacies.

Nothing ever happened.

I was invisible.

My architecture was also invisible and specific and vast and it
    faltered.

My architecture faltered in its complete originality.

I called it civic lust.

The romance of proportion was not for me.

I smoothed the horizon.

Here were the particulars of idling.

Here were the particulars of malleable proportions.

The verb was the plane of picturing.

The painter's work is horizontal.

Against history I looked and against poetry also.

I looked against space that is.

A lady's reach must exceed her grasp.

A lady must exceed space or falter.

Faltering was smooth.

This is mannerist ecology.

It was a warm September evening.

It contained old men, youths, boys, matrons, girls, domestic
animals, dogs, birds, horses, buildings and provinces.

They were properly arranged.

My technique was based on experience, not desire.

This was an ecology of distances.

I couldn't read them in the beautiful way.

What do the shoulder, the wrist, the neck, in their various
flexures desire?

What does mortal flexure want?

As a form of modest ornament, I intend to articulate
transitions.

I saw the stranger's wrist in the sugary light.
The soul is outside.

That evening, the monuments of the city were made known by
the movements of the bodies.
Each had the dignity of her movements.
Each sat at rest as pure and massy gold.
Care weighs so heavily.
Cloth is by nature heavy and falls to earth.
I wanted to describe the difference in sensation.
With grace the curtains when struck with the wind showed the
citizens.
I designed all these movements for painting.
The rooms felt patient, like concepts.
I disliked solitude and I also craved it.
I have given thought to making my words clear rather than ornate.

Then the windows were as ripe as fruits bleeding sugars.
That grace in bodies, which we call beauty, is born of sugars.
I wanted to see if my body could amend space.
Narcissus, who was changed into a flower according to the
poets, was the inventor of changing.
Some think that sugar shaped the soul.
I was lonely and hungry and civic.
I moved upwards in the sweet air.
Its simplicity or complexity was not my own.

It was a warm September evening with feminist emotion.
Motion contracted.
The air was destroying the layer of the future.
We were still sand or gravel or stone slabs.
How could I speak or groan or scream?
I did not wish to disrupt their ceremonies.
I sought the ornament of moisture.
I needed to experience radical fluid.
I played Roman games such as love, and change.

It was a warm September evening and the city and the sky were
    of the same substance.
But that substance was not in itself liberatory.
It called for abundance and variety.
I refer to largesse in thought.
You must imagine that I was standing before a window through
    which I could see everything I wanted to depict.
Utopia is so emotional.
Then we get used to it.
This work was completed in Roman Vancouver.
This is a completely original treatise.

Nothing was both new and perfect.
I saw their lives in the hospices that were their lives.
Each sat at rest as pure and massy gold.
Each had the dignity of her concept.
Some stood erect, planted on one foot, showing the face, and
    with hand high and fingers joyous.

In others the face was turned, the arms folded, and the feet joined.

Each one mounted her proper action.

Some were seated, others on one knee, others lying.

Some were nude and others part nude and part clothed.

The movements of the city were made known in the moments of bodies.

Care and thought weighed so heavily.

I speak here as an architect.

The windows became more expensive.

They were the ancient ornaments of things.

I hovered just beyond the limit of the concept.

This caused a sensation of anticipation or love.

Narcissus who was changed into a flower was the inventor of changing.

The outlines of things are frequently unknown.

The things seen fit together rarely.

I never experienced space as unifying.

Always the city was a frictional edifice.

We wanted to be happy and graceful in our work.

Because of the corporeal largesse of the century I wept.

Our freedom frightened the city.

I used to marvel and at the same time to grieve.

Other qualities rested like a pellicule over the surface of copiousness.

Still others flickered like a skin as on a living mirror.

Inside the texture of taxonomy I saw sensations.
My emotion felt like a bundle tightly bound.

There were so many things that didn't exist.
This tradition was based on æsthetic experiments.
My technique was based on desire, not experience.
I had dismantled the interior.
I was writing on the city, which was a screen on a clock.
All I wanted to do was deform a surface.
I wanted to experience the mortality of thought.
I saw no space prior to bodies and their intervals.
The secular niches flickered luminously.
Space was a very fine condition of corpuscular light.
I witnessed immaterial tissues.
I embellished antiquity with my laughter.

What is painting but the act of embrace?
I had lived subject to others, as in paintings.
Sometimes I designed finely proportioned buildings in my mind.
I occupied myself with constructions.
I was subdivided by the thought of things.
I had not fulfilled my sense organs.
A painting is soft as Narcissus.
The encompassing element faltered.
What shall I do with my senses?

On Painting

I

Pliny says it is always the season in which they are painting navies.
Not only in the church
but in your own house
the military will march
and this is equality
according to the grammarians.

The question of the origin of painting is obscure, or Egyptian.
Pliny says it had to do with combat
and victory
also known as war and triumph.
Such was its beauty
that a crow
would attempt to enter the tableau
to peck at the corpses.
We call this field of corpses
monochrome.
Its metal is iron.

A rubric is a thick red earth.

Seafoam mixed with grief becomes solid. This makes a conch shell
which is also a kind of speech.

Pliny says when the sun sets we search among rocks. Our
    tongues dry out.
The pigment called dust comes from pillage fires.

I really thought that painting would be about sex
but Pliny says it is the same as war and space.
With it we mark slaves
thus a citizen is enriched
and this is sex also.

There is a kind of chalk that gives the glow to silver.
Our grandparents used it
to draw the line of failure
behind them.

There are walls of earth.
We call this form
since they are made from moulds
composed of little panels or verses.
These forms stand for generations.

Each earth has a property and a use. Pliny speaks of each.
But generally it's worth repeating: the earth is an island mixed
    with blood.
In its furnace we concoct colour.

Pliny says that painting is necessary and commodious. It is a
    medicinal subject.

II

Now more elaborate than any style
conducted only ever unrecognizably and abhorring
and suspending the ordinary descriptions

what is painting but
The Wine of Error Daubed
on a sombre government.

III

Painting threw bricks at the police.
Painting wanted to devour skies
Satirically. Painting wanted politics
To be commodious.

Painting was severely wounded by a governmental grenade on
the Boulevard Saint-Michel in June 1968. It built barricades.
It escaped through a window. Its throat was seized by a green-
ish gas. The apparent freedom of painting will again be seized,
enclosed, stricken. Painting will be herded naked into the
street by the forces of order. Painting is ordinary. Someone
will give painting his shirt. Someone's vision will receive an
incandescent projectile. Painting cowered in its blood. This is
a secular fresco. I too wanted to throw something at them.

What can painting plead?
A string of olden coin
slung on nervous sinew
unprofitable, delirious, incredible, dear
labyrinth stitched through
with ribald sinew
Painting stuffs and swells and abhors
that circumvents
a slit of light
a fuzz of gods

A winter fur
in summer
breeding vermin

This Hyperbolical Nightingale.

The Dogs of Dirk Bogarde

I

What if I present myself to them
to quietly and agreeably confer
with happiness fretted
an aficionado of lightness
or tired openly fighting
following low tufty path through the apartment hedge
without any effortful existence
I do not continue in truth adrift
I do continue
to make it scarcely
of their play and their avoidance

In wood and feld and dale and dun, in woods
and to fields, both in field and forest, from
all directions, like a tilework
what I saw was their beau dictation
where parts grouped together at the faucet
like a shadow divine neutral
coloration work at the larynx drowsing

I spoke then as a dog that with the pale flowers groweth in the
     meadows
and into the game of speech.

They are stretched in every street
tumescent splay-foot poodles
Pradaesque – asked: do you have
– like Sir Osbert –
gout? (in the baroque)
or rather mannerist
which brought in the earnest olden
and familial atomic
blues

for a pint of honey
pours out
a gallon of gall
for a dram of pleasure
weighs as
a pound of pain
for an inch of mirth
enters
an ell of moan
shakes its collar
as ivy doth an oak
for a man to look for happiness
as fetch it
for whatever laurel is not different
sports a puffed helmet
or what happened to animals in a Europe

philosophically dying what happened
to the animals of Europe

(I
with obscurity, meditation, perfume, et cetera
with slowness and prudence, with seriousness
and accuracy and success industrially with complicity
and glut them with irremediable love while you were dying
and dryness, with disinterest and seduction and despoilment and
obscurity
with resplendence and accuracy
with reality
with accuracy
address
the byproducts
as an object clinamen

They are the twenty-seventh of twenty-nine Lucretian proofs of the
     mortality of the soul;
Techniques are stylistic.

This query meanwhile
with intervals loosened my jail-breaking sensation
without any effortful bothering
no Marxian sequence
what if I present to you – flick

the love
philosophically the sexual congress with men's languages
to the maybe there is no such thing as a female situation
I won't get used to it
being embellishment illusions
laughing

One of the humans said in his summer
You are not
the emergency of money.
A human said do you do Topiary?
As another absurdist-farcical-tragical
I say this gravely.

It was the spring of my thirty-fifth year

of raising a transnational believing class
said raising the imagining animal
or how not to break
after the ghostly simultaneous last ragged
manifesto in breath preens
flat tires of old American cars
and change breaks my heart.

The key-print of a dignity
The key-print of a dignity

Cassavetes in eighty-four describes the pact of caritas
as the natural history of the idea of guts
its trodden coloured bits
in broken asphalt alleys running creek-like
what is world but its screen tightly laced by
a hunger become worthy of turning
founded blame or sparkling befriended feminine
stray Roman dogs
the dogs of Dirk Bogarde
– what I'll call this –
understand
some slackened war

That the sense of the personal
permitting maximal referential variability
a nerve or less
enters poems using, so familiar and scandalous
utopia
chaotically histo-
arcadia
mimetically
there was scented sauntering
Homeric flowers, privilege legendary next
excellent tender
– into two equal portions –
botanical writings – their leaves slightly drying –

II

The animals of Europe went into a movie by Visconti and
    became people.
You have to hate them and their beauty also, their
Maquillage and bias-cut
Thinking.

The wood is out. We're burning bark.
Please send the animals back.
I will put them
In a *bande dessinée*
Read on the train
By a boy in a red sweater
Smelling of griffons.

They are living in their rotting châteaux like we lived in wood
cabins. Piranesi drew them living this way but some of them
don't know Piranesi. They have no water and where do they
wash their dishes. Their animals are delirious with all the
suppressed philosophy of fascism. They roll over on their
wiry backs, on their short chains, they roll in their scraps,
they grovel with humour and they can open the kitchen door
when they smell meat. They simply hopped into the truck. The
animals of Europe no longer desire synthesis.

They, antithetical, die in the heat in their kennels on their
    chains in
the draped salons of over-budget art films
Earnestly
And I plant upon them the fruit trees of the châteaux
Like anyone else
And I have simply stopped reading

One animal says to another animal it is not safe you must not
return I love you. Another says to her sister animal when you
go you will never return then she dies in a camp. Another is a
child and she stops living because of deceit. The animals in
their velvety dressing gowns have thought bubbles. They
break the incest taboo during a long cruel close-up and you
can't help but watch. The father animal is not an animal he is
a person and he is confused about money. They keep trying
to return. They are only animals. They have titles and mean-
ings. They ride trains.

Lucy Hogg by Baudelaire

I shall not pay my friend Lucy Hogg the insult
of an exaggerated panegyric
for having so successfully mastered
the affect of her pigments, nor for having
placed her figures correctly upon
the canvas. Her talent is beyond these
representational niceties. I
am commenting above all upon the wit
of her painting. I should like to attempt
to express in prose the louche structures of
her collars for they communicate a
great and mordant intent; here simplicity
forthrightness and selfless dedication
are seen marooned in ungrateful
modernity. What is it when the turn
of a lapel directs itself toward
the inevitability of genius
when a crisp neck-cloth articulates the
mortality of a concept? Yet her
wit glides beyond the sartorial, beyond
the transparent hatching of the balustrade
or urn. With sublimity it makes you
think of an extravagance of rivets
among the gilded domes; the cock
and the body and the thigh, the masses

of women in the invisible and
distant street, a density of intention
moving. It brings to life all the slow, frail
and unreliable memories in which
we display our civic charm: the slow turning
of escalators, the harmonized postures
of adolescents, the long-suffering
slope of sunlight on gentlemanly shoulders
call us into comradely if unwilling
being. Her description is too mortal
or it is not mortal. We must decide
and we giggle.

To complete this too-brief analysis
it remains for me to note one last quality
in Lucy Hogg – it is the expression
of a unique and persistent melancholy
become ornament. Lucy Hogg has
a fondness for acts of disproportion
and spatial discomfort. Her useful
instruments of depiction show awkward
joints left undisguised, the rehearsed
spontaneities of genius, ambition
and anguish themselves become instruments
so we may, upon her moot surfaces, embrace
something irreverently free blithe and
social. At the same time her surface insists

upon itself as the little poem born
of an interior, say, a studio
all crammed and gleaming with the fragments
of a hundred utopian fantasies
and tools of one sort or another.

Coda: The Device

My premise is simple. All method is a
Demonstration of history. All change
Is substitution. 'Yesterday was a
New day.'

'We are enraptured,' the stage direction says.

And why should we not live near the beauti
Ful streets, have and like the meaning of our
Pleasure and its measurement? But let us
Leave aside the question of the
Material dream, not out of tact, not
From the need to figuratively dim
Inish the little drama of sensitive
Expenditure, but in order to get
Familiar with the civic minimum.
Longueurs of desperate truancy
Name an idea about the 'un
Governable' world. Yet here I am not
Extending the maudlin fantasy of
Limits. Sure, a person will have – at her
Own admission – and penultimate
Before the marvellous environment –
Real material romance. But today I
Want to address those of terrifying

Enthusiasms and meaning's ordinary
Jobs – those for whom both origins and
Limits repeatedly fail. Oh ardent
Transgressors whose walls are also my own;
What country, good friends, what forest, what
Language is not now smothered by our sobs?

Or I could pose the matter otherwise.
What are the terms of our complicity?
We cannot definitively know, for
Reasons of faulty appearance and mis
Managed debt. Our apparent sameness
Leads elsewhere than to cause or origin.
Nor do we want simply to reverse the
Narrative, placing a cultural
Organ at an ethical height from which
'We' devolve, plying our giddy nostalgia
For the fragment. (I was thinking here of
certain æsthetics, but the remark could
apply equally to the fetishized
archive or the lust for ruins.) Is it
(perhaps) necessary to substitute
For the causal genealogies
The more ductile span of rhetoric? Though
I am, after all, trained only in
The subtleties of management, and it's
As an administrator, no, an

Administrative assistant, that I
Offer to Our Community this nod
To all who are intertwined with centres
Or the idea of 'oneself.'

I should be more precise. It is as if
History dilates the body, to pertain
To the audacity of some moral
Oblation. 'One, two, three, four, five, six.'
Consider the idea of transgression:
Its efficacy has been absorbed
By the feculent marketability
Of the skin – or should I say nostalgic
Fantasies of the skin – for who is not
Irritated by docile rotations
Of memory and hope? The affective
Passage of displacement sheds strata of
Experiment, intensity and guilt.
This detritus functions as a govern
Able material identity. The
Corpus itself, if I may risk such dis
Cretion, remains technical rather than found
Ational, and for this we can be glad.
Frankly, even our genders stutter and
Choke. Please believe that I myself claim no
Innocence from vigorous paroxysms
Of excretion: I pine for the body's

Nice parataxis, the heart's inestimable
Syntax and the good grace of your gaze; but
Here my enunciative platform borrows
A diction from judicial surfaces, which
Are also points of rest.

I shall offer a short allegory:

Imagine that a symptom is consigned
To a little known region where it
Acquires a fey materiality
With relations of obscurity
Habits of transgression and half-effaced
Myths of limitless frontier. The
Symptom takes on the historical
Function of a hero, who may purchase
For himself a plasticity imagined
As geography because it is
Visible. Perhaps this geography
Is accompanied by a people
To whom he makes the irreparable
Gift of his unique sensations of
Affective and political loss. Then
He feels compelled to move to the next
Recognizable description, befriended
By his aura of destiny. Or he
May act differently. He may dovetail

With compromise, with all that is conserved
In interiority, all that is
Simply plural, the suspect frailties
Of lack, in order to be kind. He may
Translate all that he cannot permit and
Uncover arcane explanations for
His deferred relation to the present.
He may call these dreams of broken ramparts
Walls and limits, romance or syntax or
Rubble. And what difference?

Good citizens reproduce the traumas
Of memory and transgression, thus
Guaranteeing a futurity for
Rome's citation. I myself walk towards
The fantasy of the Imperium.
I call to my sensitive friends in the
Streets: we're complicity's monuments
And the city is seriously quaint!
I believe that our complicity, like
Paternity's absurd dream, regulates
The tacit repression of history's
Absorptive convulsions. It is a gate
In the ancient style, a node where two
Spatial dispensations compete for
The iterability of an image
And its intent. We should pause at this gate

To research our emotive conventions

So that affect itself extroverts to

Articulate the commerce in margins.

Otherwise the romance between primitive

Outskirts and the Imperium stands

Preserved by the formal spectres

Of linguistic materiality

Fragmentation and doubt.

Essay on Lust

Identity can't be concise. It's knit from sequins and lust and scatters.

Mostly everyone was fucking the seven arts with a willed difficulty. Then for one day there was the collective sensation that we carried our lovely voices as if in baskets, piled up in clear tones like grapes. Each voice had achieved its particular mass.

From an interior space we heard the word *sequin* repeating in relation to leaves and the image was yellow-gold leaves moving on dark water. We had undergone an influence of death which was itself imprinted on such a moving sequin: the breath sequins, the heartbeat sequins, the organs and their slowing articulation sequins which drifting from the foreground appear to dim since they gradually go out to illuminate some event so distant we will never own the moment of its perception. But all this gives the illusion of peacefulness which is inert or at least passive when breaths burst smashing into sobbed words some urgent errand trapped in these letters as labour of light diminishing rhythm and if we fiercely decide to clear the stupid human stuff stop waiting for something to come to the father-studded earth shouldn't this impatience release itself as a tongue so new weeping stops.

In young women enamoured of their own intensities the Latin element wells up and knits from lust the pelt on the wall that's ocelot or shadepelt or the imagination of matter. Nothing's frugal. As for us, we want to give the city what lust has never ceased to put together. Young women or other women carrying their lovely voices as if on platters, their ten voices or nine voices in urgent errand dictating the imagination of matter.

It is not our purpose to obscure the song of no-knowledge.

Essay on Heaven

Heaven is probably not symmetrical. The thick black sponge lips of the hinged receptacles are the only obscenity. The entry is marked by pageantry, proverbs, slumber and embroidery.

Once a domed heaven with lights and small children dressed as angels was hung with shell-blue ropes from the rafters of the world. Cells, stars and chemicals answered each appetite. Heaven was no different from the daily protests and parties, but it was newer. Heaven knew that there is nothing directly but in form, not an emotion, nothing. Heaven showed us the erotic promise of acts of disproportion.

Now heaven seems to be constructed from famous and flagrant notional wisps and tiny-leafed material scattered through with hard green cherries or some other similarly unyielding fruit. Small pores in our skin let in daylight. Cranes slowly swing into place the massive and gently curved components of the heavenly overpass as we attend to our own commodious works, all the while speaking verse. In heaven we are free to seduce each perception or to pour doubt on it and douse it. In either case affection arises from the form at the same rate that it rises from our affluent nerves.

In regards to heaven we must also mention the dinners, travels and flowers, the studies of the flowerlike, how perfectly clear the far horizon, slow jet above the little clumps of trees in this green and that green stabbed through by the grey points of roofs. Or there is a lower flat plane in paler grey suggesting the lid of an institution. Bright plastic buckets and jumbles of bicycle wheels striped by the delicately railed metal balconies of the stucco apartment block. Foreground: bamboo fronds nearly strumming the dense lineage of service wires. Still our needs travel along these archaically twisted and ropy black lines, a skein of them loosely sewing each of our dwellings to the tall masts and thicker wires, none of them audibly humming anymore.

Let us be clear: We certainly never founded anything. Later, when it is no longer possible to remain in heaven, we will be passing over the massy shapes of the factories beside the yellow river, the shacks on the roofs of the factories, the lean-tos flanking them, the loading bays and stilted awnings all corrugated warming to rust near the rivets.

Essay on Resemblance

Our toebones resemble the toebones of another species whose individuals prefer a climate, which is also our ideal climate, the climate through which knowledge culminates in itself and in which we rest on porches because it is expedient to do so, gently fanning our digits, gently fanning.

This is about non-mystical doubling, which is also mystical. In theosophical cabins made of cedar and tin, freedom and poetry repeat unpunctuated, correspondent. Their leaves are moving.

Report 1624: The House

The House is humble and commodious. Here it is always fluent. Here we listen to voices. Here also are solid things. The House is a mould. The common division of the House is into three principal tiers – vegetal, sensitive and rational. The souls inhabiting the House migrate among levels. The inferior may be alone, but the superior cannot subsist without the other. Let this epitome suffice: the rational can not subsist without the vegetal. The House is built from this complicated love really. Repeatedly we meet its surfaces. We see the House against the long scroll of politics, which is landscape, but also the House itself is a furled scroll. In the scroll of the House we are compelled to preserve what elsewhere we desire abolished.

Ten things are framed by the House.

The first, the proportions of a young child. The second, proportions of a grown man. The third, proportions of a woman. The fourth, proportions of an animal. The fifth, something about architecture. The sixth, about an apparatus through which it can be shown that all things may be traced. The seventh, about light and shadow. The eighth, about colours, which are like nature. The ninth, about the order of the mind. The tenth, about something free, which is alone without any help from the understanding.

These are the ten things.

There is no House that does not introject its landscape of doubt. There is no House that is not a clock. We manipulate memory to make it or we dreamed its downward sloping ceilings as percussive surfaces for the sonic augmentation of rain. We wrote each of the tawdry brownish wallpapers. We dreamed the silent harms. When the porch rots we dream its decay and when the kitchen sags with the weight of our appetites it is an extremely beautiful curve. With particularity we dreamed the dry sound of pigeons' feet on the asphalt roof in summer. The clicking and grinding of the House in wind is so lively the animals won't rest. Sometimes in the House we let our outward senses sink. This is sometimes called sleep and sometimes called thought and it has to do with the economy of the House.

When asked if the House is natural or non-natural we reply: The House is strange, wayward, arcane, pedantic economics, or the House is an organ of melancholy. How are we to know if it is cause or effect, a symptom or an unease? The House is a ladder. The House has a mirror. The apple tree lifting with sparrows. Does the form of desire change? If we dilate the House the tiers of habitual emotion will be dissolved in its vastness. There will be gestures that don't complete us. There will be surfaces. When we leave the House we are light-footed.

Nevertheless
I was content to assert that atoms
always collided. Now I wonder
what happens if, as part of an
atom collides, another part does
not? Though this logic goes
against the logic of the atom, the
question remains – must
all motion be unified? Might there
be a motion that is not
itself? – Desire? Resistance?
Chance? In my perception all three
co-determine. In this way, I am not
Restricted.

Vancouver–Paris–Oakland 1995–2007

Acknowledgements

Earlier versions of these poems first appeared in *Brick, Onsets, Filling Station, Public, The Capilano Review, Fulcrum, Hole, No, Jacket, New American Writing, East Village Poetry Web, Bombay Gin, The Alterran Poetry Assemblage, Narrativity, The Recluse.*

'Lucite' was included in the anthology *Biting the Error*, from Coach House.

'First Spontaneous Horizontal Restaurant' was published as a chapbook by Belladonna in New York.

'Wooden Houses' was commissioned by the Or Gallery to respond to Carol Sawyer's exhibition *Flux*.

'About 1836' was commissioned by Artspeak Gallery for the catalogue *The Chatter of Culture*, on the work of Robyn Laba, Lorna Brown and David Zink.

'A Modest Treatise' was commissioned by Walter Phillips Gallery at the Banff Centre for a retrospective catalogue on the work of Allyson Clay, *Imaginary Standard Distance*.

My sincere thanks to all the editors, curators and artists. Ongoing gratitude also to Hadley and Maxwell for their art and friendship, and to Elisa Sampedrín and Jacob Eichert.

Poetry by Lisa Robertson

The Apothecary

XEclogue

Debbie: An Epic

The Weather

Rousseau's Boat

The Men

And Essays

*Occasional Works and Seven Walks from the
    Office for Soft Architecture*